poetry comic No. 1

Written and illustrated by

Claire Pinney

For Leo

Contents

Glorious

The view was glorious,
the wind was bracing,
with lives entwined,
our hearts were racing.

Discarded cares
and all superfluous,
the view was bracing,
the wind was glorious.

An evening in

An evening in; what bliss.
A chance to collect my thoughts and scribble this
and that and let my long-forgotten muse redress
my vacuum-headed emptiness.
Today, tonight here's hoping she will press
a faint creative thought within a crevice
of my mind.

But from the other corner of the room
persuasive voices beckon me and soon
the many hours of yet unwatched but pre-recorded costume
drama, repeated from the afternoon,
collude to steal my time and harpoon
flabby dreams of quietness. And opportune
moments fly.

I watched some footie, caught the news,
switched over then to late night Jools.
And when at last I deigned to choose
to find the wavelength of my muse,
there was no trace of that dear soul whose
alchemy I'd just refused
as night fell.

Charisma

A moth, seduced and drawn by light,
was spellbound by the charming bright
allure of comfort in the night.
Bewitched it spun in manic flight.

Enticed by such a warm embrace,
at sense and nonsense interface,
fragility in time and space,
its mind was torn like paper lace.

Too weak, too small to self-desist,
to pull away and to resist.
The bitter and ironic twist -
its freedom lay beyond the mist.

But little wings entrapped, entrain
to melodies of hurt and pain,
then round and round it spins again,
enslaved by such a sweet refrain.

Flight of fancy

Grip
manoeuvre
pivot
reach
recoil
and

f l y

suspending motion, time unspun
will she, won't she
undetermined fate, undone
truth upending, catapulting
oceans crossed and canyons vaulted
trapezing notions of reported
wistful thoughts of gold rewarded
clench, gasp
lift
a
r

r

h

flight aborted
blood inversion
head to heel deformation
arching vertebrae
innards flyaway
guts rung
pendulum swung
spinning
flung.

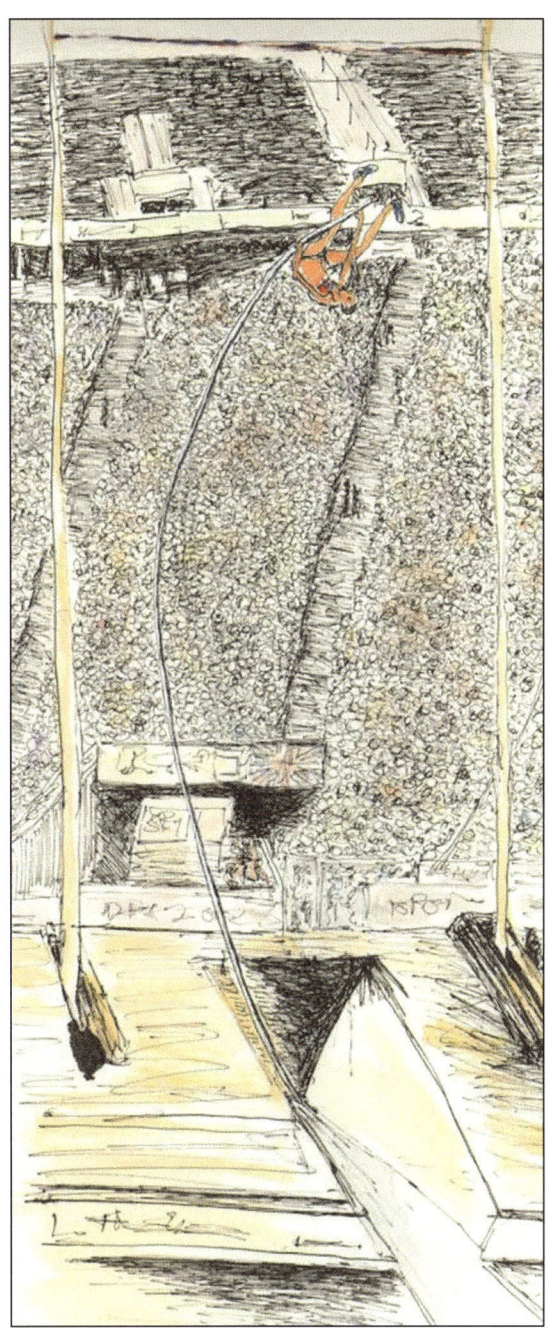

Morning commute

Who minds the gap
that widens between lives
separate on busy lines
as pathways merge
beneath the ground?

Respecting space
dividing us, I trace
the blackened wires which cling
to tunnel walls
and thread my mind

through plaited hands
and scratched, graffitied glass.
Jolted by a voice that breaks
the wall of silence,
"Stand clear", doors close.

Then on and on
while massed as one,
the multitude of journeys shared
are spent alone
in creaking tubes.

Holiday haiku

Friends on summer sand,
sparkling waves and shiny lives
to glitter Facebook.

Gutted
- an England fan's lament

A rock in the pit of my stomach,
a shattering kick in the teeth,
a gut-wrenching punch in the midriff,
the miserable smell of defeat.

I'd dyed my hair for the occasion,
dressed up like a number one loon.
Have come down to earth pretty quickly,
when hoped I'd be over the moon.

An evening lost laboured in torment,
the papers will say, "We was robbed."
I've chucked my reliable mascot
and buried my head and I sobbed.

Predictable always the outcome:
the smashing of treasured belief.
Dissecting of all that went pear-shaped
essentially brings no relief.

With injury time cataclysmic,
the referee blind as a bat,
we'd no chance of turning our fortunes;
our manager should get the sack.

I wasn't there

I wasn't there on Flodden Field
nor other sites where fates were sealed.

I didn't bring about the law
that kept your nation weak and poor.

I took no part in brutal rout
that stamped your native language out.

It wasn't me who gave your lands
into your neighbour's bloody hands.

I didn't join in Cromwell's charge,
I had no say in Rule or Raj.

When Balfour made his declaration
it wasn't at my instigation.

I wasn't in the Black and Tans,
I didn't steal your Krugerrands.

The ships transporting slaves out west
I neither launched nor even blessed.

Someone else withheld your right
to live without potato blight.

Your tribe, your race, your ancestry
I didn't touch; it wasn't me.

It wasn't me, it wasn't Mum,
it wasn't Gran or Cousin John.
It wasn't Grandpa or Aunt Peg,
it wasn't mates from Further Ed.
It wasn't Sid or Maud, I'm sure,
for they both died of phossy jaw.
But as for great, great, great, dear Uncle Bill,
God love him for his strength of will,
he gave his best for worthy cause -
for Harry, England and St George.

I'd like to draw
like Ronald Searle
(or…how I ended up doing illustrated poetry)

I'd like to draw like Ronald Searle,
cartooning life for all I'm worth,
I'll animate a blotted swirl,
inducing hoots of wayward mirth.

Cartooning life for all I'm worth,
Draw some sparkle, hopes fulfil,
inducing hoots of wayward mirth,
I'd need the wherefore and the will.

Draw some sparkle, hopes fulfil?
Perhaps I'd better think again.
I'd need the wherefore and the will
and be adept with ink and pen.

Perhaps I'd better think again…
Attempt a verse like Betjeman
and be adept with ink and pen,
inspired by wild imagining.

Attempt a verse like Betjeman…
I journey on with this in mind,
inspired by wild imagining,
or are there other paths to find?

I journey on with this in mind,
whilst hoping readers gently judge.
Or are there other paths to find?
Combine the words with sketch and smudge.

Whilst hoping readers gently judge,
the moment dawned with symmetry;
combine the words with sketch and smudge
to illustrate my poetry.

The moment dawned with symmetry!
I'll animate a blotted swirl
to illustrate my poetry.
I'd like to draw like Ronald Searle.

Commuter waltz

Not that I'm wishing to call into question your right as a ticket inspector on this busy train to insist that we all show our passes to prove we have paid for upgrading the track and renewal of rolling stock, frequently promised for this year or next by the ministers seeking to cling to their posts, not to mention the costs that are soaring for all engineering works now overrunning again; and no doubt you regret that the daily delays are the cause of a rocketing heart rate and scampering stress, so unlike your sauntering eight thirty-two, as she crawls to St Pancras where under Victorian splendour amassed are a throng of your colleagues all waiting to check once again we have paid for the intimate pleasure of squashing our noses up under an armpit for sixty long minutes and bearing in mind that you've hiked up the price for a season so soon since before, please allow me to beg 'cause though clearly I know it says 'standard' not 'first class' on this crumpled ticket it seemed such a shame when the nice seats were empty and that's why I sat here though technically speaking you're probably right that I still need to pay you the fine.

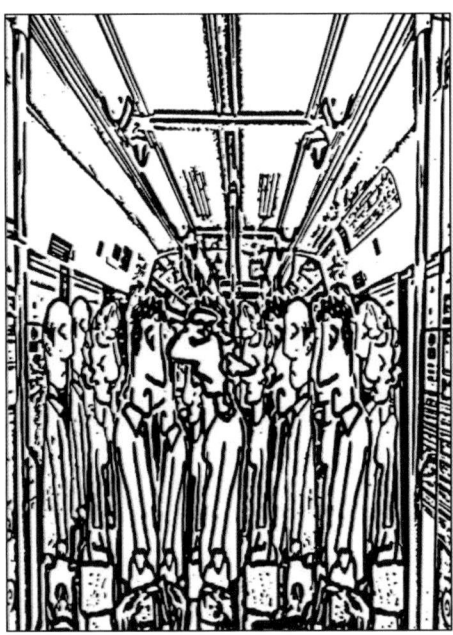

The elusive butterfly

I went in search of butterflies
whose natural residence
is found beyond our rocky cliffs
of island eminence.

A lesser-spotted butterfly
of stunning quality,
exquisite in its finery
and woven tapestry.

I wanted to experience
its bright exuberance,
I wanted all the beauty which
it bore in elegance.

And so for years I watched in hope
but one thing was conclusive:
for all the time and money spent
this creature was elusive.

Till finally it dawned on me,
there was one thing I lacked.
I couldn't see the butterfly,
my telescope was cracked.

Observations

After stubbing your toe on the leg of my chair,
"I did that on purpose", I heard you declare.
Then happy you'd hid any sign of a wimp,
you manfully left with a bit of a limp.

Lunchbreak

I wish I wish
I'd filled my head with poetry.
Instead
I scraped my flimsy thoughts over
shards of breaking news
stories
and wondered why
the hour's toll had torn
my soul.

ALONE

ALONE,
I've settled.

Outside the
Winter lashes

but no longer
bites.

Mystery

Where do you wonder wool runs to
when the ribbed, winter warmth
that was your sock
works its way into webbing,
wrestling then wrenching your toe,
till it's winched in a woven noose?

Surely it slid to the same shrouded somewhere,
secretly luring the string from the signage,
enticing the knots that seemingly
held things so stoically
strapped to the railings,
till the last strand slipped away.

There no doubt sped the thread,
thickened by times it was thimbled through
buttons on thermal-lined coats,
then gradually thinned to a thong
that dangled pathetically,
threatening to drop on the pathway.

Likewise I never saw love take its leave,
for it lingered then leaked
to a limitless galaxy
where dare say it lazes in some sort of landfill,
loitering idly with effortless languor
with wool and string and thread.

Survivors

Fold up the blankets and pack them away,
hands off my giblets and clear the buffet.
We'll pour the l'orange in a glass of champagne
and drink to the future with hope once again.

The cranberries we'll crush and the croutons we'll share
with friends at the pond when we party down there.
By hook or by crook, we dodged all to survive,
three cheers for the veggies who kept us alive.

Organic Matters

You said, "Organic Matters",
So I Fed the Hedgehog
Not Slugs Nor Grubs,

but cabbage,

Naturally Grown.

Biodynamically.

And He Lived Healthily
till Lured by Succulence
of Worm and Wheat germ

Fat From a Field, Fertilised,
and He became Less Hedge,

More Modified Hog.

Genetically.

Till He grew Large
and Slow of Speed
to outrun Four-by-Fours.

Indeed,
it's true For all,
but For some,
More so –
organic Matters.

Pigeon post

My prayer took off with pigeon post which caught
the wind in slipstream heading southward over dunes
and under wing, whistling onward to the coast.
And there, perched on a lobster pot he pondered long,

the message tucked against his breast he'd borne
    'cross borders to the sea,
        forged in frantic hope and launched by fingertips, this plea
        had sped with purpose swiftly through the skies
            and landed here

where nothing rushed, nor rallied to respond in time's quiet cove.
As water lapped on landing stage and harboured boats,
        he pondered long that pigeon post.

Dreams of a would-be revolutionary

Brothers, sisters, now's the time,
forward march, link arms with mine.
Rise as one to change the world;
see our banner's star unfurled.

Grab the moment, seize the day,
growl a little on the way.
In hearty voice our gallant troops
will overcome the men in suits.

Suddenly a thought occurs…
what if no-one joins or worse?
Passers-by might jibe and mock,
making me a laughing stock.

Then there's the question of the law,
I've never been in jail before.
The sentence might be very long…
Wait! Did I leave the gas on?

Better go back home and see,
hope I haven't burnt my tea.
Don't get me wrong, I'll join the fray,
tomorrow is another day.

Something stirring

Something is stirring
but what, who's to say,
unsettling the leaves
in a strange kind of way.

Winds from beyond,
pervading with force,
creating the southbank,
corrupting the north.

Weaving a path
through a disparate world,
ambition defracted
and dreaming deferred.

Whipping up wodges
to stuff in the bank,
while a million CVs
first floated then sank.

The just about managing
strummed a sad song,
but great were the parties
in flush Albion.

Utopia

Utopia arose and shone in skies
above my head, her towers scraped the clouds;
a model built on hope and stacks of lies,
with new design to rouse the sullen crowds.

The people's wish will be embodied now.
We can create from this dark mass, this void,
from nothing, something, fresh and free of doubt;
a vision cast, a life reborn, enjoyed.

But in my mind I know, my eyes have seen
a place where someone stole the dream.

Terror

The day stretched out before commuters, tense,
head down, and purpose led. The platform crammed
with workers' sluggish shoulders pressed against
a narrow-minded missionary of damned
hatred. And this his creed, his one intent -
to tear apart and mutilate this land.
He detonates his load and lives are gone.
A sacred cull, a martyr's kingdom come.

Amid the slaughtered stricken innocents
this blind ambassador of cruelty lies -
a testament to bitterness prevents
one child to see, to say his last goodbyes,
to breathe. Then stories of the grim events
soon echo to a fallen world that cries.
As culture reels assaulted, butchered for
a primitive belief and festering sore.

The Legend of the Three

Boldly in the belly of the beast we rode
that warm and wistful afternoon
when the world was ours.

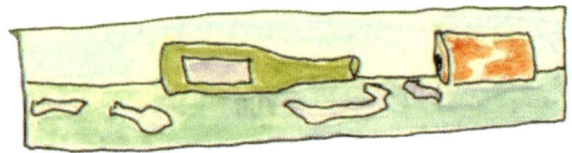

Twas skimming the scumcrust laketop,

brandishing our swords of faith,

Fire in our hearts and Fire Fuelling our dragon's roar,

We plunged to pierce the deep and found imprisoned wherewithals

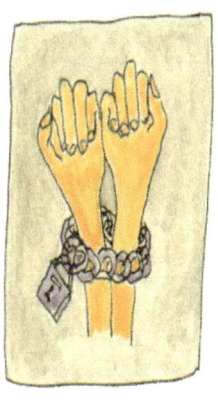

and dreams, that once danced dutifully to others' schemes,

Were Freed to life and liberty,

So goes the legend of the three.

Transformation

Tethering yourself with me
I am made new…etymologically.
No longer an unfitting ewte;
transfigured, I'm reborn a newt.

What happens when the flip is true,
unstuck, renounced, the great undo?
From lofty heights where once a nadder,
I shrivel to a common adder.

Notions of essential change,
with one's status rearranged,
illusory or just a fudge,
a numpire soon will be the judge.

Words to break and resegment us,
plus, divide, deplete and minus -
the rebracketing of thee and me,
splitting ontologically.

The etymological process by which some words evolve is sometimes referred to as rebracketing, false splitting, faulty separation or resegmentation. Over time an ewte became a newt, a nadder became an adder and from the word numpire we now refer to an umpire.

Embers of hope

In vaulted halls of sacred order
alone she stands with her Creator,
petitioning the Lord of grace
and martyrs of her childhood faith.
No small mite to shelter hope -
savings in an envelope.
Grafted through the scrapes and knocks
and dropped into the candle box.

Star

From diverse worlds where shadows creep
and drawn from waters running deep,
we do not fit a mould or stencilled norm,
nor are we fashioned blithely to conform.
We are unique in brilliance,
and colourful resilience,
as varied as the melodies
from lullabies and rhapsodies.
And from our captor's net we were released,
that night we saw a star rise in the east.

The vicar's wife

The vicar's wife creeps to the shed,
"to clean" she said,
busy in the garden
should the flock call by.

The vicar's wife takes to her bed,
"to rest" she said,
wrapped in woolly duvet
when the flock call by.

The vicar's wife downs a sherry,
a sling with cherry,
and all that's necessary
if the flock call by.

US
CHiCKeNS

Here We live on this plot, two souls - comfy spot.

Hatched, matched, idly trot,

grain a-plenty, wanting not.

Time flew, tick tock,
ushered in plucky lot —

Pan cook, sizzle wok,

Hot pot!

Stress

Squeeze an inch
the extra space
to breathe
or pinch
with elbows out
and filling up
no room for sense
or doubt
instead a shove
he went to work
once mindful
then berserk.

What the monkey saw

Uninvited, whispered power,
come the moment, come the hour.
A mind released, a loosened pen,
for dissidents, both now and then.

The eye that couldn't help but see;
the ear that heard belonged to me.
You thought you held a tight control
but not my breath, my will, my soul.

The monkey saw, he also heard
and now will speak of, word for word.
A signal from a source unknown,
the trilling of a whistle blown.

The whoopsie do

A dog had left a whoopsie do
right there for all to see,
just up from King's Cross station and
nearby RNIB.

As luck would have it pavements here
are wide to some degree.
Most dogs pull owners to one side
and piddle up a tree.

But this one probably was a stray
and did his 'excuse me',
immensely brazen, on our path;
a crime most would agree.

We all stepped over, or around,
alertness was the key,
just up from King's Cross station and
nearby RNIB.

This morning Colin's train was late;
his thoughts were all at sea.
He had to stand from Hendon and
had cramp below his knee.

When stepping out on Euston Road,
he loved his MP3,
at peace thanks to the comfort of
his favourite CD.

Which meant his powers to scout around
for dangers in his way
were predisposed to concentrate
on songs by Doris Day.

"Que sera," her voice rang out,
"Whatever will be, will be."
Just up from King's Cross station and
nearby RNIB.

The World
in a bubble

Circling Within a Fragile bubble

And pressed by an ocean of necessity,

It's the little things of beauty that sustain

a delicate existence

of sheer grace,

held together by routine

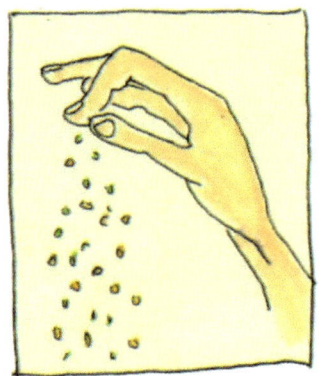

and breakfast flakes.

Printed in Great Britain
by Amazon